THE NO-NONSENSE DIVORCE HANDBOOK

A PRIMER FOR BUSY PARENTS

CAMILLE CARDELUS

CONTENTS

Chapter 1

THE DON'TS LIST

WE CAN ALL MESS THINGS UP...

We start with the basic pointers that, irrespective of how much you know about divorce, will be important throughout the process.

- Don't assume that divorce will be a battle. However, don't assume it will be a breeze either. Be alert and prepared. Some individuals change drastically when confronted with the process.

- Don't act impulsively. Everything you write, say or do can be used in court. That includes text messages, social media posts, photos and emails. All is discoverable by the courts.

- Don't assume that the court will show sympathy. Perception, eloquence and positioning can be more important than reality. Also, keep in mind that you will not have a lot of time to testify since family courts handle many cases. You will have limited time with the judge. Laying out details and complexities is not as easy as you may think.

- Don't take it personally if others are not appalled of what happened and happens to you (lawyers, the court). They see many cases. As bad as your case might be, they have seen worse.

- Don't be threatened by the lingo. Legalese has its own way, however, it is just the use of fancy words. A kid is "a child," custody is "possession." See past that. Keep this in mind when you read Chapter 3.

- Don't block your spouse from seeing the children. Seek help immediately and consult with a lawyer if you are worried about your or your children's safety.

- Don't tell your spouse you want to divorce until you know what divorce entails. Once divorce is filed, the spouses are subject to several restrictions. Also, you need to ponder the implications of your spouse filing first. Sometimes the spouses are eligible to file in more than one court. The court that gets the case first, usually decides it. If your spouse beats you to filing, you could be at a disadvantage if:

  a. The court is far from where you live (had you filed first, you could have filed in a court closer to you)

  b. The laws of the court where your spouse filed protect you less

- Don't think about what your spouse would think of you; think about what you need to do for your well-being and that of your children.

- Don't isolate yourself. Now is when you need help the most.

- Don't trust that your family and friends will save you. You will save yourself, with their help.

- Don't think that your lawyer will do all for you (unless you want to pay a lot!).

- Don't let what is going on at home impact your job. It is your lifeline.

- If possible, don't leave the house. Not having a place you can call home makes the journey more difficult. If you have kids and you leave, you could be thought of as someone that disrupted the family or as someone unstable. You could also be charged with kidnapping.

- Don't be alone with him/her, when you tell the news. Pick a public place.

- Don't tape, videotape or record conversations without consent of the others taking part, even if you are one of the persons participating. Depending on the state, doing so might be illegal. Taping, however, can be necessary and life-saving if facing a situation in which you are at risk. Talk about it with your lawyer.

- Don't break the law. What can be done or not done during divorce can be tricky, stay tuned to what your obligations are and respect the rights of others.

- Don't get so deep into your own emotional distress that you miss the stress your children are going through.

- Don't do research or calls about divorce on shared or unprotected devices.

- Don't use the kids, protect them.

- Don't lose your cool. I don't mean that you cannot get mad. You just cannot lose your cool or be hysterical. It is the hardest. Some spouses use their husband's/wife's "instability" to build an outrageous case against them.

- Don't use this book or any generic advice as a source of truth. Each divorce is unique. Many things in this book, including this don't s list for example, could be wrong or incorrect for your case.

- Don't divorce without hiring or at least having access to a lawyer. They can be expensive, but you need, at a minimum, counsel.

- Don't believe what your spouse says. Believe what your spouse does.

- Don't let yourself sink emotionally to the point of becoming inactive. Do your part. In time, you will know exactly what happened.

- Don't let revenge or anger guide your decisions. Focus on building a future.

- Don't leave your yoga, God or whatever gives you peace; now is when you need that the most. You need something to remind you that divorce is a long moment, and long moments also pass.

Chapter 2

Before Filing for Divorce

Are you ready?

Ending a relationship and filing for divorce are two separate decisions. Before filing for divorce (or before responding to your spouse's request to divorce):

- Go through this list to see where you stand, but DON'T do anything until you discuss each item with your lawyer.

- Read Chapter 3, the Divorce Process. It will empower you by giving you an understanding of what will happen.

- Define what is important to you. Is it the kids? The house? Being away from him/her? Try not to focus on the now. Visualize where you want to be in six to twelve months.

- Read the legal limitations that will apply from the moment that the divorce starts through its end (each state has its own set of rules, usually known as the divorce "Standing Orders", you can easily find them on the web). Unless you go to court to modify them, those rules govern your life while the divorce proceedings take place. For example, the rules might limit your ability to spend money on non-routine expenses.

- Think about your access to funds. Some spouses do horrible things once divorce filing happens or they suspect it is about to happen, even when they are not allowed to do so. Some change online banking passwords. Others simply take all the money.

- Make sure you have a fund you can claim your own to cover living expenses and legal fees.

- Know that blocking your spouse from funds is a bad idea. Once divorce is filed, you really cannot change anything without making sure it is legally ok. For example, if you hired and paid someone to cut the lawn, you may not be able to cancel that service even if you no longer live in the house.

- Know that legal fees will strain your budget. Think about how you will face this challenge. Leave pride at the door. You may need to sell assets or the help of friends or family. Beware of using credit cards. Divorce expenses pile up at exorbitant speeds.

- Safe ward important documents (your passport, immigration documents, marriage certificates, home documentation, contact lists). Purchasing a safety deposit box at a bank is recommended.

- Understand how you can freeze your credit cards. It is important not to block your spouse. However, you also need to ensure there is no abuse. Talk with your lawyer about this item.

- Keep track of the household expenses, who pays what and how much, starting a few months before the divorce. This document will help you have your spouse contribute to the household as he/she did before the filing.

- If you are the breadwinner or contribute economically to the household, talk with your lawyer about it. In theory, as the divorce occurs, you need to make funds available immediately to allow the continuation of the household maintenance, even if you are not living at the family home.

- Make a list of all the items that you might need to change, but that you cannot without your spouse's consent. For example: If you have a joint mortgage, you will need your spouse's consent to refinance. If you are considering moving, you will need your spouse's consent to move the children. Discuss these items with your lawyer before filing, so that they are timely addressed.

- Develop a plan to let your spouse know:

    a. Would you do it by phone? By mail? By courier? In person? It is recommended that you are not alone, particularly if there is a history of emotional or physical abuse. Doing it in a public space might be the best option.

    b. Where would you do it? Where would the children be when you tell him/her?

- Decide how and when you will give the news to the children based on their age and maturity. Consult a family psychologist if needed.

- Define living arrangements for you and the family.

    a. Female spouses tend to leave the house, even before filing for divorce. Please consider staying and asking your spouse to leave. It might be daunting, but it can be your best option, especially if you have kids. After you file for divorce, you can request the court to grant you exclusive use of the home too, but such request should be based on real fear and danger. Discuss your options with your lawyer.

b. If your spouse insists on staying but stops helping or causes an ill environment, document it and consult your lawyer.

c. There are instances where moving out is the only option. Perhaps staying at home, even if your spouse is not there, is troublesome. Before moving out, consult with your lawyer and still consider going to court to explain your situation. Moving out with the children without the consent of the other parent can have severe consequences.

d. Leaving home sometimes has no consequence. However, if your spouse is belligerent, you need to think about how he/she will frame what you did to get whatever he/she wants.

• Prepare a suggested schedule for your spouse to see the kids. The chapter about child custody and support provides additional pointers.

• Evaluate if there is risk of your spouse taking the children, with or without your consent, to a different country. Also evaluate if you would like to do that while the divorce proceedings take place. Consultation with a lawyer with knowledge of international family law is paramount. Not being informed can have severe consequences.

• Consider creating a new email account to correspond with your lawyer and clearing your passwords from all home devices.

• Delete your spouse from your 401K, life insurance beneficiary lists and your will before filing for divorce. After filing, you may not be able to do so as freely.

• Before the process starts, ask for help. What are you going to do about child care, errands, meals and transportation?

- Talk with your employer and explain your situation in a professional and composed way. Use good judgment to define the best time to have this discussion. If you have a good boss, he/she will support you. If your boss is bad, make sure a colleague and another member of management you trust are aware of your situation.

- If you feel comfortable with it, talk with your kids' teachers, and perhaps the school counselor, so that they can help while your kids are at school.

- Organize and compile all documents you will need to build your case during the divorce.

- Have your phone memory cleared so that you have enough space to video-tape a situation, if needed for your safety. Remember that video-taping or taping conversations without consent might be illegal, even if you are participating in the conversation.

- It is hard, but if you are not emotionally available or irritable, have someone that you love, who is level headed and trustworthy help the kids and you "walk the path." You need to pull yourself together and be strong when you see your kids. Some individuals seeking support fall into a romantic relationship immediately. Every case is different, but be aware of these relationships often resulting from a misplacement of emotions due to your vulnerability.

- After thinking about all the above, schedule a meeting with your lawyer. Share your concerns or plans, which might inform how, where and when he/she feels it is best to file for divorce.

Chapter 3

THE DIVORCE PROCESS

ALL WILL BE OK.

You are about to read a succinct, yet fairly comprehensive, description of the divorce process. The content is a bit heavy, but not rocket science (do not let the lingo or level of detail intimidate you!).

As you read, you will be tempted to think that the divorce process is "too hard." It is not. You are simply being exposed to a lot of empowering information.

Capitalized words are defined in the glossary.

The typical steps to divorce are:

1. Decision to divorce.

2. Consider working with a lawyer.

3. Lawyer search and selection (interviews, high level advice). Legal representation can be retained in different ways:

   a. If you are unable to afford legal representation, a pro-bono lawyer could be available to you through charitable organizations or other non-profits (Chapter 5, Lawyer Selection, provides some useful links).

b. For simple divorces (where the spouses agree on everything) some lawyers charge a flat fee. Fees vary and can go from $200 (to fill out certain forms) to more than $3,000 (where a bit more support is needed).

c. For more complex divorces, you usually have to sign a retention contract. This document details your lawyer's services. It also provides the hourly rates that lawyers, clerks, paralegals and secretaries will charge. Within this format you deposit to a Trust Fund. For example, your lawyer may ask you to deposit $1,500 to the fund. As your case progresses, the money will run down to, let us say, $750. At that time you will be asked to replenish the fund back to the $1,500 balance. Law firms usually bill monthly. The bill details the time your lawyer spent in your case, and what activities he did. Hourly rates can be anywhere between $150 to $450 for each hour of the lawyer's time.

4. Understand the advantages and disadvantages of filing the papers first, especially if the case could be filed in more than one court. The court that receives the case first usually decides it.

5. Find out what court has Jurisdiction over your case. You cannot file in just any court. You or your spouse have to meet defined Residency Requirements, 6 months in Texas, for example. You also need to file in the right court. There are likely several family courts in your state. You need to figure out which one corresponds to you. Keep in mind that a court that has Jurisdiction over your divorce, does not necessarily have Jurisdiction over your kids. The place where the kids have lived in the previous six months, or the place to which they have Substantial Connections usually has Jurisdiction. Sometimes two courts have Jurisdiction at the same time. Your swift and thought-out filing strategy could make a huge difference.

Depending on where filing happens, you may or may not need to travel to solve your case. Also, some states have better (or worse) divorce laws.

6. Discuss with your lawyer the likelihood of you having an Uncontested Divorce (you and your spouse agree on all items and you will just put everything in writing and validate the document) or a Contested Divorce (you and your spouse do not agree, as a result, the court may have to decide for you).

7. Decide the type of divorce you will file, Fault or No Fault Divorce. Some states do not have a Fault Divorce option.

8. Analyze if the Standing Order works for you (default rules that apply the moment you start the divorce process).

9. Decide if you need to file a Protective Order at the same time that you are filing for divorce.

10. File the Divorce Petition. Filing means that you or your lawyer are officially starting the Divorce Petition process by giving documentation to the courts.

11. Serve divorce papers to your spouse. Service means formally notifying your spouse that you have filed for divorce. You can informally notify your spouse and have him/her sign a Waiver of Service, which saves you the hassle of using a "Process Server" (the person that has the power to do a "formal delivery", which is usually a deputy or sheriff).

12. Let the "Waiting Period" run. The Waiting Period varies by state (it is 60 days in Texas). During this time, the spouses try to work out agreements regarding custody, division of property and the like. You can get your first court Hearing at the end of the Waiting Period (if the court's schedule so permits it). Divorcing may take longer than the Waiting Period. It all depends on your divorce characteristics and the court's

schedule. If one spouse is misbehaving or not respecting the Standing Order, a Hearing for Temporary Orders might be needed before the actual divorce Hearing takes place.

13. As the divorce proceedings happen, having a lawyer is very helpful. A lawyer can recommend how to respond or not respond to inquiries, actions or communications from your spouse or your spouse's lawyer. Lawyers also use legal tools and communications to make sure your spouse complies with court Temporary Orders or the Standing Order. During the Waiting Period, information exchange requests take place. These requests follow rules and procedures that are already set. The spouses must respond to information requests within specific time periods. Each lawyer can do a request for the following (some of these can be objected while others cannot):

a. Disclosures, Rule 194 (Texas). This document asks that you share general information such as: Who represents you, which experts you have consulted, and the names of all persons with knowledge of relevant facts (your witness list).

b. Admissions. This item is not as common. If your spouse is lying, this tool will assure that inaccuracies are on record.

c. Written Interrogatories. A document where multiple questions are asked, particularly about your work and your assets. Questions have to be answered under oath.

d. Production and Inspection. A request to provide tangible items for review.

e. A Sworn Inventory and Appraisement (valuation). A list and description of what you and your spouse own, and who should own each item after divorce. The list has to be updated as things change.

14. After information has been exchanged, the spouses can reach agreements through:

    a. Spouses/Lawyers' direct discussions. If an agreement is found, a Settlement Agreement is written. The lawyers then transfer the agreements to the document that will be validated by the court, which is the Divorce Decree.

    b. Mediation. The spouses ask for the help of a neutral third party (legally authorized to do so) to find agreements and finalize the divorce.

15. Before a Mediation session, a good mediator will ask to receive beforehand from each spouse:

    a. Their overarching positions (Do you want the house? Full custody? How much economic support is requested?).

    b. Basic information about income and living expenses.

    c. A Settlement Offer including from each side:

        i. The kids' custody arrangement (Possession) and the rights and duties that each parent will have over the kids (economic support, health care obligations, rights to decide for the kids, etc.).

        ii. The amount of Child Support. State laws vary and define the minimum and maximum amount a spouse shall give to support a child.

        iii. The amount of Alimony (money to support the other spouse). This is only applicable if the receiving spouse is unskilled and other requirements are met. Not all states have Alimony.

        iv. Insight on the issues that are most important.

    v.   Insight into special circumstances.

    d. If successful, a Mediated Agreement is signed and a Divorce Decree is drafted.

16. If the negotiations or mediations do not require the help of the court to decide matters, the judge only validates the Divorce Decree (which was written based on the Mediated Agreement or the Settlement Agreement) and orders the spouses' divorce. Usually only one of the spouses needs to go in person to the court, while the other just signs.

17. If the spouses do not find agreement, the court intervenes. A Hearing or multiple Hearings are scheduled. Based on evidence and testimony of the parties, the Judge then decides the final outcome. A Divorce Decree is also drafted, but has portions that reflect the court's decision.

18. After the Divorce Decree is signed and finalized, the judge declares the couple officially divorced.

    a. In some states, divorced individuals cannot remarry until after a defined amount of time has passed.

    b. If the Divorce was reached by court decision (not by a Settlement or a Mediated Agreement), the spouses can Appeal. The Appeal is only available if the spouse finds that the law was applied incorrectly.

19. Following the stipulations of the Divorce Decree, additional documents are signed to ensure the transfer of property:

    a. Warranty Deed. Transfers the property of an asset (usually the home) to one of the spouses.

    b. Deed of Trust to Secure Assumption. Filed on the official public records office of your location. This clarifies who is to pay which debt. It also protects the spouses if one of them defaults on a mortgage that was under the spouses' names before divorce, but is supposed to be paid just by one spouse after divorce.

    c. Power of Attorney to transfer motor vehicle. Document that gives a person the authority to sell (transfer ownership) of a car that is titled to another person.

20. Also based on the Divorce Decree, the Child Support and Alimony accounts transfers are set up.

21. Once you are officially divorced, you and your ex-spouse will perform the obligations within the Divorce Decree.

22. As obligations and rights are performed, it is important to keep a calendar to track Visitation and Child Support timely payments.

23. Motion to Modify, if needed, for example, to increase Child Support or change the Visitation schedule.

ADDITIONAL STEPS FOR INTERNATIONAL DIVORCES

1. Consider consulting a lawyer with experience in international family law if you are divorcing a foreign national, you are a foreign national, your children are foreign nationals, or the U.S. is a foreign country for you or your children. An international divorce expert will:

    a. Assess the validity of your marriage if you married abroad.

    b. Evaluate the enforceability and influence of a foreign Prenuptial or Postnuptial Agreement.

    c. Give you an overview of the steps you need to take to validate your divorce abroad (particularly Child Support and Visitation).

d. Alert you about Jurisdiction and child abduction risks.

e. Help you analyze which court has or could have Jurisdiction over your children.

f. Advice on how you could help or hurt your case if you or your spouse take your kids abroad or move (that type of movement can create a Jurisdiction mess).

g. Advice you about the impact of divorce on the immigration status and on nationality matters of the family members. Consulting with an immigration attorney is recommended.

h. Connect you with a lawyer licensed to practice in another country, especially if such country could claim Jurisdiction or applicability of its law to your divorce.

2. If there is a need to validate the divorce internationally:

a. The Divorce Decree needs an Apostille (a seal from the U.S. State Department validating the document as official).

b. The Divorce Decree also needs to be translated. Translations have to be performed by translators approved by the foreign country.

c. A lawyer licensed to practice in another country will have to do Exequatur or a similar process over the Divorce Decree (validation of U.S. Decree in the foreign court).

Chapter 4

SHOULD I HIRE A LAWYER?

HECK, YEAH!

Several books and websites describe a process called "Pro Se Divorce" (in other words, doing your divorce without a lawyer), however, even when short of funds, I recommend hiring a good experienced lawyer because you need:

- Expertise. Your lawyer will have experience with similar cases; he/she will also have access to lawyers with more seniority to seek answers to difficult legal questions (Chapter 5 provides guidance on how to select a lawyer).

- Access to draft materials. Writing a Divorce Decree is complicated. The proceedings and intermediary legal documents are also tricky. The web has several do-it-yourself templates. That being said, only a reputable lawyer or law firm will have clauses that are not present in simplified documents.

- A filter. Divorces are emotional for you and the ones that love you. A third party that knows the court process will help temper down swift reactions. He can also draft your messages in a more neutral tone. He/She can convey positions that could be difficult to assume by you.

- A third-party observer. Your lawyer will experience the complications of your divorce. As such, he/she will be able to "vouch" for issues caused by your spouse.

- Help. Your lawyer and lawyer's clerks will fill out, organize and file court documentation. For a working parent with kids, these services are life saving. Going back and forth to the court is not fun.

- Independent work. Some couples hire the same lawyer. The strategy can work, but it is risky. Sharing a lawyer can lead you to concede more that what is fair.

- Cost reductions. Legal proceedings can start by being simple. However, complications arise. You might double your expenses by hiring a lawyer late in the game.

If after the above you still prefer the do-it-yourself route, please consider having a one-time consultation with a lawyer, a paid one if possible (so that you get genuine advice and not a sales pitch). Give a lawyer the opportunity to explain the pros and cons of not hiring a lawyer, based on the characteristics of your case.

Chapter 5

Lawyer Selection

WHO SEEKS SHALL FIND.

Some lawyers give complimentary consultations. However, paying for a first meeting is not a bad idea. A paid lawyer is usually more open to giving high-level advice during that first meeting.

Each lawyer works differently. There is a variety of prices based on reputation and experience. Lawyers can work independently or within a firm. The benefits of working with a law firm are:

- There are backup lawyers if your lawyer gets busy.

- Usually there are several levels of experience in the firm. If needed, your lawyer will have access to a more experienced lawyer.

- Sometimes the costs of the lawyer's trips to the court are lower if his/her firm goes there all the time.

- Many think that independent lawyers are more humane. There are also humane firms.

Picking the right lawyer or firm is tricky. I remember interviewing an excellent lawyer. She was great. I could see that she cared and that she was extremely competent. The price was right too. There was a problem though: My case required significant support and collaboration with international lawyers. As much as I liked her, I decided to hire counsel from a firm instead. I needed to know that my lawyer had access to experts and support.

As you make your choice, think about resources, experience, money, empathy, maturity, and chemistry. Beware of those that feed off your pain or your need for redemption. Also be wary of lawyers that ask you to sign a retainer agreement without giving you time to think.

Below you will find several questions you may want to ask. Appendix 1 includes links to lawyer search sites and pro bono (free) organizations. Similar organizations exist in every state.

- Why did you choose to do family law? Is it your specialty or part of your practice?

- How long have you been practicing family law?

- How will you charge me for your services?

- What are your firm's hours of operation? If you are on vacation, how many lawyers of your experience does your firm have? Will they pick up my case?

- Can you please give me a short walk-through of the steps you follow when resolving a divorce case?

- How long does a typical divorce case, with no major issues, take to resolve?

- How many lawyers are in your firm? Will a lawyer with a bit less experience handle my case at times? If so, will I be charged a lower fee for the work performed by him/her?

- Do you have assistants or paralegals that do part of the legal work? If so, what types of tasks do they perform? Would a lower fee be charged for his/her services?

- How much is your retainer? Is there a minimum amount of funds I need to keep at all times for you to continue working my case?

- Will you pay court fees, transportation, copies, etc. from the fund? Will I be billed separately for court fees?

- Will your team take all needed files to the court?

- Based on the description I gave you, what are the challenges and outlook you see for my case?

- After knowing a little bit more about my case, can you please give me some guidance on how many hours would be needed to solve my divorce? I am just trying to define what my total cost would be. I want to be prepared so I do not have to change lawyers due to a lack of funds.

- Will you be the lawyer leading my case? Will I be speaking with you most of the time? Lawyers usually work several cases simultaneously. They do not usually work on details and standard documents (they have paralegals for that). How long the lawyer has worked with his paralegal can be an indicator of how strong his team is.

- Would you be available after hours in case of an emergency? Does your office have an emergency hotline? What do you consider an emergency?

- Do you have a policy regarding the maximum time you can take to reply to a client inquiry?

- Does your firm do pro bono work?

- How would I communicate with you and how often?

- Based on the information I gave you, what would be the strategy we would follow for the divorce? Do I have a chance to achieve the outcome I hope? Why or why not?

- What costs, other than legal fees, would I incur?

- If needing to consult with specialists on certain legal topics, what are your connections? Are you able to consult with more senior lawyers within your firm?

- Unfortunately, the fees from a lawyer with your level of expertise are very high. Is there a possibility for a lower lawyer that you trust to handle my case and consult with you as needed?

- Do you have connections with law firms in other countries?

- Has your firm handled international divorce cases? If so, with which countries?

- International divorces sometimes go to state or federal courts. Is your practice able to represent me in those courts too? Within which states are your counsels licensed to practice?

Chapter 6

WORKING WITH YOUR LAWYER

EACH MINUTE COUNTS...

Divorce is stressful. Having to communicate in the midst of a crisis is tough. As you talk with your lawyer, keep these points in mind:

- Email subject lines are important, use them wisely.

- Long emails are usually read last.

- To the point summaries rock! Details help.

- Calls are to solve issues and need to have an agenda (inclusive of a list of the topics you want to cover and an objective to achieve).

- You are one amongst many cases; make sure your concern is always clear and memorable.

- Paralegals (staff that assists your lawyer) can be great helpers. Make sure they know you.

- Being organized pays off (if you have an inbox that receives tons of email, it might be a good idea to set up an account that is devoted to your legal conversations only).

- Your lawyer can draft everything, however, only you will know if what is written is right. Do not overlook reviewing documents you receive.

- You can reduce costs by drafting some items yourself (found a Visitation schedule you liked on the web? Edit it and send it out!). A lawyer drafting from scratch will take more time than one reviewing or editing suggested content.

- Send emails to your lawyer that include your preferred solution.

- Always copy your lawyer's paralegal. Communicating with him/her instead of your lawyer sometimes helps, especially if you are looking for status reports about your case.

- Be selective about when you email your lawyer. If everything is presented as an emergency, your lawyer may not be responsive when a real emergency occurs.

- Always send in writing your explanation of events and then have a call:

  a. Your lawyer charges for his time. An explanation over the phone takes longer. When you explain items in writing, usually you cut to the chase and give the most important details only. Also, you are able to explain everything without interruptions.

  b. A conversation over the phone should always be about what you and your lawyer can do. A back and forth via email takes a long time. It is faster over the phone.

  c. When you share something beforehand and then schedule a call, your lawyer is supposed to prepare for your call. Do not be disappointed if your lawyer shows up unprepared. If he/she does, he/she at least will read your message then! You are suddenly at the top of his list.

d. You pay in 15-minute increments (usually). Optimize your communications. However, do not compromise. If something is important, it will be worth paying for the advice.

e. Lawyers are usually busy, but they should be able to reply or acknowledge your communications within 24 hours. Scheduling productive calls will be key to ensure there is consistent progress in your case.

The templates on Appendix 2 can help you draft different types of emails to communicate with your counsel.

Chapter 7

WHAT YOU HAVE AND WHO GETS IT

WHAT IS MINE IS YOURS. WELL, MAYBE NOT.

Each state defines community property (the things that belong to both spouses) differently. As a general rule, go back to your marriage documents (including any Prenuptial or Postnuptial Agreements) to figure out how your marriage was set up. No mention of division of property does not mean that everything is owned by both parties.

If there is nothing about property on your marriage documents, you are subject to the standard rules of the state where you got married. There are two types of states: Community Property states and Equitable Distribution states.

1. Community Property states:

    *   Their assumption at marriage is that the community property (marriage property) belongs to both spouses, independently of who earned or bought the property.

    *   Community Property is to be distributed equally between the spouses (absent a Prenuptial or Postnuptial agreement, fault or other attenuating circumstances).

    *   In general terms (with some exceptions), gifts from one spouse to the other, inheritances and property that was separate before marriage are not Community Property.

31

The rest is, even if acquired under the name of one spouse.

2. Equitable Property states:

- Equitable property means that each property is owned by the person that earned such property (this usually means that you can trace who purchased the asset or that the asset is property of only one of the spouses).

- The typical assertion is: What is in your name is yours, what is in the other spouse's name is his/hers.

- Equitable Property states are to distribute joint property in a "fair and equitable" way (commensurate with the circumstances of the divorce).

- You can go to court and try to prove that there was a verbal agreement to create joint property, but it is difficult to do.

On the topic of property, there are several nuances. A lawyer is definitely needed to clearly know the property set up of your marriage, and the rules that apply to your divorce. Despite the state rules, you and your spouse can agree to something different, especially if you do not want to sell, but just want to keep one thing or the other. That said, rocking the boat away from the state rules is not easy. Before negotiating, be well aware of how the split would be according to the rules. Questions to keep in mind are:

- Is what I owned before getting married still mine alone, but what I purchased after I married owned by both? What if I mixed what I had before marriage with what I earned after marriage?

- What if I was purchasing via credit something before I got married, and my spouse helped me pay that debt after I got married?

- What is the validity and interpretation of my Prenuptial and/ or Postnuptial Agreement?

- Am I divorcing in a Fault or No-Fault Divorce state? In some states, a spouse's misconduct in certain areas might alter the division of property. That said, the chances of getting a better deal because your spouse was in fault are low.

Once you address the above questions and compare what you want with what the state rules say, you can decide how much you want to negotiate.

Using the courts to get sworn inventories helps. Many individuals hide assets or debts. People think twice before hiding assets if the court is involved.

The list below provides major categories to consider as you build inventories of your and your spouse's assets and liabilities.

ASSETS

- Real state property

- Cash accounts with financial institutions

- Accounts receivable (money you or your spouse are owed, e.g. state income tax refund)

- Businesses owned

- Retirement accounts

- Company retirement benefits (pension, profit sharing, 401K)

- Military and government retirement benefits

- Other deferred compensation benefits

- Life insurance and annuities

- Publicly traded stock, bonds and other securities

- Motor vehicles (boats, water craft, airplanes, cycles, cars, trucks, etc.)

- Household furniture, furnishing and fixtures

- Sporting goods and fire arms

- Antiques, artwork, and collections

- Electronics and computers

- Clothing, jewelry, and items of personal adornment

- Livestock

- Club Memberships

- Frequent Flyer mileage accounts

- Miscellaneous assets (intellectual property, licenses, crops, cemetery lots, gold or silver coins not part of a collection, tax overpayments, loss carry-forward deductions, deductions)

- China, Entertainment items, other

- Trust, Estate and Custodial assets

- Assets held for either party as fiduciary or beneficiary

LIABILITIES

- Attorney fees

- Other personal fees resulting from defending the case

- Credit cards and charge accounts

- Federal, state, and local tax liability

- Claims that encumber property or assets

- Mortgages

- Vehicle loans

- Other liabilities

- Student loans

As with all the other divorce decisions, you and your spouse can solve everything via negotiations, mediation or through the court (Appendix 3 provides negotiation tips).

When everything is final, the decisions are captured in the Divorce Decree. If a transfer of property is needed, your lawyer will help you get the appropriate signed documents.

CONSIDERATIONS FOR INTERNATIONAL DIVORCES

You may need to verify the laws of your country of marriage. You or your spouse could claim that the laws of such country are the ones that should apply in respect to property division.

Chapter 8

CHILD CUSTODY AND ECONOMIC SUPPORT

STEP ONE, BUY A CALENDAR.

In respect to the kids, the ultimate outcomes of divorce are the Possession schedule and the Child Support arrangements. Absent special circumstances, both apply to kids below 18 years old most of the time.

Capitalized terms are defined in the glossary.

WHAT ARE THE RULES WHILE EVERYTHING IS BEING DECIDED?

After divorce is filed, and while the divorce is resolved or finalized, the Standing Order defines the rules of the game. Parents usually have to stay close to what was habitual to the children. Keeping that "normality" during divorce is not always possible. If things get ugly while the divorce process is going on, one of the parents can ask the court to issue a Temporary Order that addresses the issues.

WHAT IS THE PROCESS TO DEFINE WHICH PARENT AND WHEN EACH PARENT HAS THE CHILDREN?

When solving custody matters, courts are to decide matters in "the best interest of the children." To avoid misinterpretations of what that means, each court usually issues what is called a "Standard Possession Order" or "standard visitation order" (a standard

Visitation schedule created by the courts). This order is the default standard solution. The document usually exists in two versions: One that applies when parents live relatively close and another that applies if the parents live far from each other. Some states have Standard Possession Orders that differ depending on the child's age. In Texas, for example, the Standard Possession Order assumes that one of the parents spends most of the time with the child, while the other visits. Some states have a special Standard Possession Order for children under three years old.

As the divorce negotiations outside of court advance, the parents may decide to adopt or modify the Standard Possession Order. Shared custody or splitting the custody of the children, unless agreed by the parents (and even when agreed), requires more work. There are templates, but not as detailed.

The "Standard Possession Order" is the top point of reference. The court uses it as a benchmark, however, the court also recognizes that each situation is different. In some instances one parent is sure that the order is inadequate, while the other claims it works. If the parents can't agree, the court intervenes to decide. The court takes upon itself making sure that the outcome is "in the best interest of the children." In many cases it assigns you a child custody evaluator. This person can visit the parents' houses to assess the situation and give a recommendation.

As you think about the Visitation schedule, ask yourself:

1. Are all children under 18 years old?

    a. Yes

    b. No. Children above 18 years old no longer have a Possession schedule.

2. Who will have the kids most of the time (primary party)? Select one.

a. Parent 1

b. Parent 2

3. Based on your above answer, the primary party is [Parent 1 / Parent 2], visiting party is [Parent 1/ Parent 2]

4. Do you have children under 3 years old?

    a. Yes. There is usually a different Standard Possession Order for little ones under three. It is important that you think about this. If having multiple kids, are you ok with one child seeing the visiting party more than the other?

        i. Yes. You can rely on the different Standard Possessions Orders more.

        ii. No. You will need to create your own schedule to assure a balanced Visitation.

    b. No. No need to worry about this one.

5. Are you and your spouse living around the same area (less than 100 miles, rule varies by state, consult with your lawyer)?

    a. Yes. In these cases, the primary party is usually required to live within a certain radius to keep the agreed upon Possession Order in effect. E.g. if the primary party moves to a different state, he/she may lose certain rights or acquire certain obligations (for example, the visiting party might not be obliged to go pick up the children from the primary party's home any more; instead, the primary party might need to travel to a middle ground or to the visiting party's domicile to render the children for Visitation).

    b. No. The Standard Possession Order has different terms if the parents live more than 100 miles away of each other. As you consult with your lawyer, you might need to look at this option. The primary party might be permitted to move more easily without giving up rights or acquiring obligations.

6. Would you like different rights defined if one of the parties commences to live more than 100 miles away (distance varies by state)?

    a. Yes. Then you need to review the rules of Visitation that would apply or design your own schedule.

    b. No. Even though there exists a Standard Possession Order for parties that live more than 100 miles apart, you can agree a Possession schedule that works irrespective of distance or that incorporates special circumstances.

7. Are you going to permit/request video/phone Visitation?

    a. Yes. In Texas, there is no specific order for this type of Visitation. If you consider this option, you may need to create your own schedule (day of week, duration, etc.). Many parents agree very loosely, just indicating that they will give reasonable phone/video access.

    b. No. Your Decree can be silent on the topic. However, keep in mind that not permitting electronic or phone access could be viewed unfavorably by the court. Courts can also view unfavorably excessive calling or extreme access demands.

WHEN IT IS ABOUT THE CHILDREN, WHO DECIDES WHAT AFTER DIVORCE?

Figuring out the Visitation schedule for the kids solves one of the biggest issues: Who stays with whom and when? The next step is defining who decides what. Depending on what the parents agree or what the court decides, a parent may:

- Decide all the time

- Decide only when he/she has the children or

- Not have decision rights at all

For example: When married, you and your spouse could independently permit your kid to have a non-emergency surgical procedure. After divorce, it might be only one of you who can authorize such procedure.

The assumption in Texas, and other states, is that after divorce, both parents should have the same rights and obligations towards the children. However, that is seldom the case. Usually, the parents agree or the court rules that one of the parents will have exclusive decision rights over certain topics. This does not mean that one of the parents is the "Sole Managing Conservator" (a fancy name given to parents that really decide everything exclusively). It just means that the parents are "Joint Managing Conservators" (they both have rights and obligations), where one of the Conservators could have more rights than the other.

Extra-curricular activities fall in a special category (music and sport lessons, for example). A parent can enroll the children in any activity he or she wants, as long as the activity takes place during his or her Possession time and does not put the children in danger. There is no penalty to the other parent, if he/she does not take the kids to activities that he did not enrolled the kids on, unless this disrupts the children's education or development.

WHAT ABOUT THE CHILDREN'S ECONOMIC SUPPORT?

Although Child Support will be one of the most critical and contested pieces of your divorce, it is the easiest to figure out (in the end, it is just a number). States usually have specific formulas and maximums per child that will apply (there is not much negotiation here). This chapter will just give key pointers.

Child Support is usually calculated as a percentage of income and it tends to be recorded as a fixed amount. If your spouse does well in the future, you are stuck with what was calculated when you divorced. Due to this phenomenon, even after your divorce has been signed, you can request a review of the amount by doing a Motion to Modify later on.

If you are negotiating outside of court and have the opportunity to influence how the support is included in the agreement, asking your lawyer to write a sentence like "Child Support of $[a number] monthly or 25% of the spouse's net income, whichever is higher" could save you a lot of headaches. You still might need to use the court to enforce changes, but at least they would be already documented (state limits could still apply).

A final note: Some people do not know the true base salary of their spouse. One key benefit of going through the courts is that you will get insight into his/her income level.

WHAT ABOUT MY ECONOMIC SUPPORT (AS AN EX-SPOUSE)?

Here is where we talk about Alimony, "a husband's or wife's court-ordered provision of funds to a spouse after separation or divorce." Simply, Alimony is a stipend that one spouse gives to the other. This support can be temporary (while the kids grow up, while the spouse acquires skills to work) or permanent (if the spouse is disabled, for example). The basic requirements vary by state. For example, in Texas, a person could be entitled to Alimony if, among other factors, this person had been married with the other more than ten years. It is hard to get. Lots of justification is needed.

An important note on Jurisdiction (State and International)

Determining which court decides kids' matters can be difficult. Even though one court might have Jurisdiction over the divorce, that does not mean that such court has Jurisdiction over the children. The simplest rule is: The court of the place where the children have resided the past six months (or the time required to comply with the Residency Requirements) has Jurisdiction. Things can get complicated. Even if the children have resided in a place for six months, one of the parents can say that such place has no Jurisdiction. There is no black and white rule. What if a parent moves the children from one location to another without the other parent's consent? If you have international Jurisdiction issues or if the divorce and the kids Jurisdiction are not the same, it is advised to consult with a specialized lawyer. Most of the time acting quickly is critical.

Where the kids were born, where they lived and even to which place the kids have Substantial Connections can define which court decides matters. Always keep in mind that your recognition of a court (you replying to it, as if recognizing that it has Jurisdiction) can be your first step to a good outcome or a bad one. Sometimes contesting the Jurisdiction of a court might be your best action. Keep in mind that two countries or stares could claim Jurisdiction over a case simultaneously, each based on its own laws.

Chapter 9

CONTENT OF THE DIVORCE PAPERS

YIKES! IF ONLY I HAD THOUGHT ABOUT THAT THEN...

The final divorce papers (the Divorce Decree) will define your and your family's schedule and interactions for a long period of time. Even though your lawyer will take care of the document, you need to know what goes into it. As with anything, mistakes could happen and things could be overlooked.

The final Decree (written in legalese) is a document based on a template that lawyers or law firms have created over time. As such, the document contains new clauses that will throw you off, because they were never explicitly discussed. Do not panic, it is normal. The only thing to remember is that "normal" or "standard" does not mean that you should blindly sign it. Always read the document and ask questions, especially if the Decree was not drafted by your own lawyer.

If you go through Mediation, you will sign a Mediated Agreement (kind of formal, but still with some things agreed on the fly and drafted with little detail). That document is then used to draft the Decree (the real thing), which has more detail and which will contain a lot of the standard language that lawyers are used to include.

The following pages provide an extended list of items that go in the divorce papers.

GENERAL

1. Choice of Jurisdiction. At the time of the divorce, the spouses might have lived in the same state. Over time, one of them can move. By choosing beforehand the Jurisdiction, you avoid a spouse filing for modification in a place that is far away from you, if the law permits it. A spouse's move does not mean he can file and resolve everything from his new residence. However, it complicates everything. Keep in mind: A court that can solve some divorce matters, could well not be able to solve child custody matters (there are special rules that pertain to child custody and support).

2. Choice of law. Clearly indicate that the Divorce Decree or Settlement Agreement is "governed, constructed, construed and interpreted" according to the chosen law. This makes sure nobody changes the rules of the game if the Divorce Decree is reviewed by a different court. Also indicate under the laws of which country and state the agreement is signed.

3. The Divorce Decree is what counts. Indicate that the Divorce Decree supersedes any other agreements previously made.

4. Debts. Clearly specify obligations to pay and requirements to cancel or liquidate joint accounts.

5. Divorce under seal. Agree that the divorce will not be in the public records (divorces are usually public matters).

6. Drafting. If you signed a Settlement Agreement or Mediated Agreement, one of the lawyers has to take care of putting the content into a Divorce Decree. Usually, you will choose your lawyer to do the drafting. Include a clause indicating that the parties also agreed on the draft.

46

7. Effect of Prenuptial or Postnuptial agreements. State that the Divorce Decree has precedence over any Prenuptial Agreement or Postnuptial Agreement.

8. Expenses. Specify who pays for the attorney fees and other fees.

9. Property. Stipulate obligation to transfer ownership of property by a defined date ("Special Warranty Deed"). Establish deadline to vacate the marital residence and to assume possession of assets.

10. Taxes. Indicate who pays for them (for the period that both spouses may have ownership of the home or owned a business) and who can claim tax breaks from mortgage interest payments. Specify which of the parents can claim the Child exceptions within his or her tax return.

11. Testament or will. Sometimes it is hard to track all the places where one has put a spouse as beneficiary. This clause clearly indicates that the spouse is deleted from any will or testament.

12. Alimony. Applicable at times, depending on the length of the marriage and the cause of divorce.

CHILDREN CUSTODY

1. Change of residence notification. Obligation of parents to report, to the court and to the other parent, a change of address as soon as it occurs.

2. Residence restrictions (if one parent gets custody most of the time, the standard is that such parent cannot move so easily, or at least without the court's permission).

   • The Standard Possession Order has standard residence restrictions; parties can make them stronger or weaker.

This is particularly important. A parent's move impacts who does what and the kids' pick-ups and drop offs.

- Drop-offs and pick-ups. The Standard Possession Order makes drop-offs and pick-ups the responsibility of one Conservator or the other. The parents can agree that it is always one of the parents doing pick up and drop off. It can be agreed that drop off and pick up always take place at your house, or you can agree a mid-point (at home is recommended; if one parent is late, the other just waits at home).

3. Mediation. Clause that indicates that the parties will use first Mediation to modify the Conservatorship, Possession or economic support of the children. Note: Going to court for lack of Child Support payment must not require Mediation first.

4. Out-of-state travel. Depending on risk, sometimes you may want a clause that requires parents to provide authorization if the kids are traveling out-of-state.

- Each parent shall share the details of the children's trips (when, to where, how long, which cities, with whom, address, phone, flights, if the parent will be absent at any time, etc.).

- The parents can also agree the number of days of advanced notice needed to let the other parent know about the children's travel.

- If a parent causes costs to the other by not giving authorizations or passports on time; that parent shall be liable to the other for the incurred losses or costs.

5. Undesignated periods of possession. Specify which parent will have the children when the Decree does not specify who has the children.

6. Extended periods of Possession. The Standard Possession Orders usually give a full month for the children to be away with the visiting parent. The parents can agree that the parent that will not be with the kids can have them one weekend in between.

7. Right of first refusal. If one of the parents cannot exercise his/her possession (is absent 24 hours or more); the other parent has the right to have the children.

8. Child care. Right to know who is taking care of the children (contact information and ability to talk with such person).

9. Children's birthdays. Assure that the dates work (avoid Standard Possession Order causing conflict) and that both parents can see the children that day.

10. Basic needs of the children. Require Conservators to have all necessary furniture, clothing, etc. A Conservator can have the right to verify the same by adding a clause to the Divorce Decree. You can even request receiving a video before the visitation schedule starts.

11. Will the parents use the Standard Possession Order? The Standard Possession Order usually works for older kids; significant modifications may be needed for kids that are zero to three years old. You may also have special circumstances that prompt you to seek modification.

12. Notice of sex offender. Each parent has to notify the other if he/she marries or lives with a registered sex offender.

13. Communications (electronic and phone). If neglected, this can be a source of controversy, perhaps important to agree the minimum/maximum frequency, duration and timing.

CHILD SUPPORT

1. Child Support amount. There are some requirements by law; the parties can agree to a higher amount. Salary, Trust Fund income and other types of income are part of the base to calculate Child Support.

2. Child Support duration. By law, it is until 18 years old in general; however, the parties can agree a longer period.

3. Earnings withholding to cover Child Support. Stipulate that support is going to be withheld from the paycheck of the person giving support. The person giving support shall also pay a Monitoring Fee from the government.

4. Child Support after death of parent. Child Support continues after death using the assets or state of the parent that died and was giving support.

5. No credit for informal payments. Parent has to pay Child Support through the pertinent government agency. Such parent shall not be able to claim deductions for expenses that he/she has outside of the withholding. Any such payment or expense is in addition to the support.

6. Parent to pay for expenses during divorce. Specify and detail expenses that a spouse might need to reimburse the other because he or she did not contribute to the sustainment of the children while the divorce process was taking place.

7. Life insurance of the parent providing Child Support. Require that the parent giving Child Support gets life insurance so that support can continue after his/her death.

8. Specify that a parent giving support must do all processes necessary to ensure compliance with his support obligations.

9. The parent giving Child Support has to report any change of employment to the disbursement agency and has to make the necessary changes so that disbursements are made in a timely manner.

10. The parent providing Child Support must ensure there are no delays on payment of support due to change of employment or other reasons.

RIGHTS ON CHILD

1. Who decides what after divorce? Usually it is one of the parents (sometimes consulting or informing the other parent). Topics that require definition (legally and practically) are:

   • Who decides the children's education (school, etc.).

   • Who manages the children's wealth.

   • Who will represent the child on legal proceedings that are related to him/her.

   • Who decides if the children can or will take psychological or psychiatric inpatient/outpatient treatment.

   • Who manages the earnings of the child.

   • Decisions regarding child's medical procedures.

   Each state's civil code includes additional items that need to be addressed.

USE OF MEDIATION

1. Resolution of parenting conflict using Mediation and/or alternatives that include negotiations outside of court. Ensure that individuals participating on the collaborative process do not testify if the model does not work. On the collaborative process, the parties usually hire collaborative lawyers and a

neutral psychologist. If the process does not work, the parties can agree that those going to trial are not the same as those that participated in the collaborative model.

HEALTH CARE MANAGEMENT

1. Indicate who pays the children's health insurance (usually covered by the person that does not have the kids most of the time).

2. At least one of the Conservators must be obliged to purchase health insurance or put the children under his work insurance (sometimes it is better to put the kids under the insurance of the parent that has the kids and have the other parent reimburse the premium). Make sure the item is mentioned. An omission presumes the primary Conservator provides insurance.

3. If a parent reimburses the other for insurance premiums, make sure that the Decree does not have a fixed amount, but that the amount changes if the premium amount changes.

4. Specify the split for other health care expenses. How much of the cash health care payments are covered by each parent? The split is usually 50/50. Indicate the time within which the parent owing the other parent needs to pay. This is to cover co-pays, out-of-pocket expenses, prescriptions, etc.

5. Meaning of "health care". Make sure that health care does not mean only medical care, but also psychological, dentist, orthodontist, etc. All of it, routine and extraordinary.

INTERNATIONAL TERMS

1. Validation of divorce abroad. Define who is responsible for executing the process, which might include Exequatur

(validation of one country's judgment in another country) of the Divorce Decree.

2. Define who pays expenses incurred for international processing and procedures.

   • Translation and Apostille (validation of the Divorce Decree by the State Department) of documents.

   • Legal fees from foreign courts and lawyers.

3. Collaboration to complete paperwork of the children in regards to their dual-citizenship, if applicable. In some countries, the signature of both parents is needed for administrative matters.

4. Passports.

   • Specify who controls them and who will have the children's passports most of the time.

   • Obligation for traveling parent to give back passports within a defined timeframe.

   • Court order indicating that one parent can request the kids' passport to the government without the presence of the other parent or indicating that the authorization of the other parent is needed. Each country has its own rules. It does not hurt to try to put some order to this topic, especially if the children can get passports from different countries.

5. Prevention of child abduction.

   • Assertion that a given country is the country of habitual residence of the children (documented as agreed by the parents). This is important; the place of habitual residence defines the court that has Jurisdiction if you need to use international law to solve problems.

- Require non-traveling Conservator to sign authorization for travel.

- Inclusion of standard forms to request and provide authorization for travel.

- Consider prohibiting the children's travel to countries that are not part of the Hague Convention.

- If needed, Bond from traveling parent, which can be used to fund legal fees in case of abduction.

- Require Exequatur of Decree on country where the couple originally married or where the other Conservator lives or is from:

  a. Exequatur shall indicate that the United States is the country of habitual residence of the children.

  b. Stipulate that a parent can deny authorization to travel if a parent is traveling to a country that is not a member of the Hague Convention (which gives protection for cases where there is child abduction).

6. Child Support payments. If a parent moves to a country where the agency helping with payments is not present; the parent with the obligation to give support has to make sure payments continue. Obligation of parent to ensure withholding also occurs in the foreign country.

7. Waiver of other rights. Some countries have laws that can be invoked and cause problems. For example: In France, Art. 14 and 15 of their civil code or Articles 42 through 48 of the French Nouveau Code say that French citizens can bring a lawsuit against any person in France. The clause is not used and the law itself has been hostile to it. However, not having a waiver could cause unnecessary issues and legal procedures.

For example, a French spouse married to an American could file for modification of the Divorce in France, even when neither of the spouses has lived in France for the past ten years. The case would be farfetched, but it would require a legal response.

Chapter 10

INTERNATIONAL CONSIDERATIONS

DAMN IT! ZUT! DEMONIOS!

Those words came to mind when I realized the amount of international issues I had to handle. The good news is that divorce in the global world can be done. Here a few things to consider before filing in the United States, when you, your spouse or your kids are not Americans:

1. Discuss with your lawyer the likelihood of dual Jurisdictions and the validity of your marriage.

   - A marriage that took place in a foreign country is usually valid in the United States. Filing for divorce usually does not differ in process.

   - In general terms, you are to divorce in the place that you or your spouse resided and reside for a set period of time (those are the places that have Jurisdiction). Caveat: Some countries can claim Jurisdiction if one of the spouses is of their nationality.

   - A court with Jurisdiction over the divorce does not necessarily have Jurisdiction over the kids. When international matters get in the mix, things become more difficult. Very few lawyers are fully familiar with international procedures and rules. It is important for you to consult a specialized lawyer, even if it is for an hour. In the simplest cases, both spouses accept the Jurisdiction of one court, even if such court claims Jurisdiction "loosely." In the most complicated cases, both spouses contest the Jurisdiction. A spouse can even claim that the decision of a court is invalid because it had "no Jurisdiction." This becomes further complicated as some countries might have an inclination to support their own nationals. International law and specific Jurisdiction determination rules exist (across state lines and internationally).

2. Define, with your lawyer's help, which Jurisdiction is the one that should be preferred. In general, if dual Jurisdiction exists, the first Jurisdiction that hears and decides the case usually gets to control everything. You may want to act fast, unless you want to defend your case miles away from where you live. But what if the case is heard simultaneously by two courts? The court that decides the case first could have an advantage. It could seek enforcement of the judgment in the other court (usually the court of another country or state).

3. In some instances, you can have your case heard in one country but applying the laws of another country. Discuss this situation with your lawyer. This is particularly important if you married abroad. The definition of community property and separate property might be different where you got married. Also, the rights over your spouse's property may vary depending on what law is used.

4. If you have a Prenuptial or Postnuptial Agreement, investigate its enforceability.

5. Once the above has been considered, make sure the Divorce Decree includes:

- An acknowledgement that the kids' residence is where they live. This is important as the Hague Convention (an international treaty that sets rules and provides some legal backing to recover children that have been abducted by parents) bases a lot of its actions on the definition of which is the habitual residence of the kids.

- If there is high risk of child abduction, include a Bond requirement (a monetary kind of insurance your spouse has to buy each time that he/she travels abroad with the kids). The Bond is only used to cover expenses you may incur to recover the kids.

- A notice and authorization requirement each time the kids are to travel abroad (inclusive of flights, dates, who is traveling, if the kids will be without one of the parents at any time, and destination).

- A clause blocking the kids, unless authorized otherwise, from traveling to countries that are not part of the Hague Convention.

- Passport control clauses.

  a. State who shall hold the passports most of the time.

  b. Indicate when the passports have to be given to and returned by the traveling parent.

6. The Jurisdiction and law that shall be used going forward (if you are able to agree on it). This clause does not override the Jurisdiction requirements that apply to each state. However, if there are two places that have Jurisdiction, your pre-agreement for one helps.

7. Once your divorce is finalized by the U.S. court:

59

- Translate and Apostille your Decree, so that it can be used and validated internationally.

- Get Exequatur of the translated document in the country of your interest. This process will validate the U.S. court decision in another country.

International divorces usually entail taking additional steps, including using the below documents, as needed:

1. Stay extension request of foreign family member. A spouse that suddenly starts to be alone might need help from family. Those family members might live abroad. The Stay Extension Request is a petition to the United States Immigration office to permit a family member stay longer than his/her visa-allowed stay limit.

2. Opposition to children's passport issuance. If risk of abduction exists, you might want to oppose to the children being issued passports. This is applicable for countries where one spouse can request a child's passport without the consent of the other.

Appendix 4 includes a stay extension request and an opposition to children's passport issuance template.

Consulting an immigration lawyer is critical if you, your spouse or your children were born outside the United States.

Chapter 11

WHAT IS NEXT?

FULL RESET? NO. JUST THE BEGINNING OF A NEW CHAPTER.

Being legally separated certainly marks a new phase. However, divorcing does not erase or fix it all. As you transition to your post-divorce life:

- Take time to recharge and heal your soul. The legal process directs emotions to a specific self-preserving outcome: Being legally disconnected from your spouse. After that outcome is achieved, there is much emotional and practical work to be done.

- The same way you informed yourself to have the best and most peaceful divorce process, seek information and professional counseling to find the best path to build a new better life.

- Remember that your goal is to build your own life, not to build a better life than the one of your spouse.

- If you have kids, the journey for them will be difficult. Focus on them. Read books about the impact of divorce. Devote time to observing your children and being tuned in to what they are feeling.

- Some couples can have respectful interactions after divorce. Others cannot. Do not hesitate to request legal or co-parenting counseling if you and your ex-spouse are unable to cooperate. Also don't forget to track how well or not the visitation schedule is working (Appendix 5 lists some tracking tips).

WORDS OF WISDOM

READY, SET, GO!

Life after divorce is the continuation of your journey. Embrace your story with the good and the bad. Forgive and love yourself and others. Look forward. Live fearlessly.

APPENDIX 1: LAWYERS, TRANSLATORS AND APOSTILLE

RESOURCES TO START THE QUEST.

LAWYERS

Useful places to scout for lawyers:

1. International Academy of Family Lawyers

   • https://www.iafl.com/

2. American Academy of Family Lawyers

   • http://aaml.org/

3. Super Lawyers

   • http://www.superlawyers.com

4. Legal aid and Pro-Bono Texas (no cost or reduced cost lawyers and resources)

   • https://www.justia.com/lawyers/divorce/texas/dallas/legal-aid-and-pro-bono-services

TRANSLATOR

Certified Translation Dallas

2310 N. Henderson Avenue Suite A

Dallas, TX 75206

214-821-2050

Fax: 214-821-7065

http://www.certifiedtranslationdallas.com

APOSTILLE

Contact useful in Texas only. This store can obtain the Apostille in 24 hours.

The UPS Store in Downtown Austin

815 Brazos St. Suite A

Austin, TX 78701

512-476-5316

Fax: 512-482-0457

store0233@theupsstore.com

https://austin-tx-0233.theupsstorelocal.com/products--services/apostles

APPENDIX 2: LAWYER COMMUNICATION TEMPLATES

TEMPLATES ROCK!

TEMPLATE 1: REPORT CONCERN

Subject: [Urgent] [Topic] [Your case number and name]

Dear _____

I am experiencing a situation that I cannot handle myself. It is in regards to[__bold font__]. Please find further down the issue details and context, along with my thoughts on the topic. I appreciate your advice. Perhaps we can discuss over the phone at X or X on MMM DD? [or request here for a specific action].

[Sorry for the urgency, please call me as soon as you can.]

Kind Regards,

Name

Email

Phone Number

Issue:

[Write Here]

When:

[Write Here]

Where:

[Write Here]

Others present or not:

[yes/no]

What happened:

[Write Here]

My concern:

[Write Here]

My proposed solution:

[Write Here]

TEMPLATE 2: CORRECTION OF FACTS

Subject: [Urgent] [Topic] [Your case number and name]

Dear _____

I saw a few inaccuracies on his/her lawyer's letter that I would like to correct via a formal communication. Please find further down my thoughts. I am curious about your recommendation and timeline to reply. Perhaps we can discuss over the phone at X on MMM DD?

Kind Regards,

Name

Email

Phone Number

Inaccuracy
Example: His/her lawyer says that I do not let him/her see the children.

The Facts
Example: He/She has called, and I have said I cannot talk at the moment. But it is because I am really busy with school and work. I cannot stop the daily routine easily.

What I would like us to do
Example: Could we ask him/her to formally set a few times? I do not want him/her to call when he/she feels like it.

[Write in bold your brief position. It might be all your lawyer will read. You can write more but write it on regular font. Make sure that the sentence in bold is concrete.]

Additional Background

Please see detailed descriptions below (attached)

[Your lawyer does not have time to read emails that are three pages long. Even if he/she does, it will cost you a lot of money. By putting appendices, you still provide the support information in an organized way.]

TEMPLATE 3: REQUEST FOR AN UPDATE

Subject: [Urgent] [Topic] [Your case number and name]

Dear _____

I just wanted to touch base. Have there been any developments? As of our last communication, below is the status I am aware of:

- Fact 1

- Fact 2

I was wondering if [Fact 1] had already been [sent/approved/received] and about our next steps? Any line of sight regarding timing will be extremely helpful. [Perhaps we can discuss over the phone at X on MMM DD?]

Than you in advance,

Name

Email

Phone

TEMPLATE 4: SENDING DOCUMENTS

Date: [MMM DD,YYYY]

Subject: [Urgent] [Topic] [Documents attached]

Dear ____

Please find attached the following documents:

1. [Document Name].

    a. As of [MMM DD,YYYY]

    b. [Original/Copy]

    c. Contents: [Write Here]

    d. Comments: [Write Here]

2. [Document Name].

    a. As of [MMM DD,YYYY]

    b. [Original/Copy]

    c. Contents: [Write Here]

    d. Comments: [Write Here]

Please let me know if you have any questions.

Kind Regards,

Name

Email

Phone Number

FAX COVER SHEET

Date:_____

Time:_____

Number of pages (including fax cover sheet): _____

Fax To:

Name: [Write Here]

Phone: [Write Here]

From:

Name: [Write Here]

Phone: [Write Here]

Subject:

[Write here]

Description of contents:

[List documents sent here]

Comments:

[Add any comments you may have]

APPENDIX 3: SUCCESSFUL NEGOTIATIONS

WIN WIN... MEH.

The ideal negotiation ends with everybody winning. Unfortunately, that is not always the case. Devote time to your strategy (even if it is only thirty minutes).

To succeed during a negotiation: Be aware, be diligent, have foresight.

AWARENESS

When you negotiate:

- Spend time visualizing the scenarios you could face and what you would say.

- Negotiate with yourself beforehand. Play both roles in the negotiation. Doing so will help you better value what you bring to the table. The exercise will also highlight your strengths and weaknesses.

- Know that you are the owner of your time. Creating artificial deadlines is one of the most used negotiation tactics. When facing time constraints, always evaluate if you can ask for a longer deadline, do a counter offer or break the bluff by walking away expressing openness to re-engage.

- Do not let fear or emotions get to you. Causing harm to others is not the goal. Allowing harm to yourself is not the goal either. Do not let pride or the wish of ending the marriage ASAP limit your ability to do what is best for you and your loved ones.

- Remember that:

  a. Business is always business. Divorcing is not *business*, but you need to keep realistic expectations. Keep track of or check your priorities regularly. Focus on what will mean something objectively, not emotionally.

  b. There is always a right way to say things. Learn and practice how to say no, how to say yes, how to diffuse aggressive behavior and how to walk away in a calm way. Use your emotions as needed (sometimes showing a bit of frustration is the right thing to do); do not let your emotions use you. However, if your spouse is abusive, even if you say things the right way he/she will likely respond abusively. Make sure you are in a secure public place when discussing sensitive matters.

  c. Trustworthiness has to be at the center of your every action. Your credibility is at stake every step. Bad actions during negotiations outside of court will act against you in court.

DILIGENCE

Beyond personality and negotiations experience, successful dealmakers excel in preparing. When you negotiate:

- Do your research (a LOT of research).

- Know what you want and what your spouse mostly wants.

- Be aware of your venue setting and its impact on the negotiation.

- Choose the right type of interaction (in writing, in person, over the phone?).

- Know your BATNA (best alternative to non-agreement). It will tell you when it is the right time to walk away or change strategy.

- Have a plan. The plan shall include a purpose (what do you want to get out of the negotiation?), an agenda (what items are you going to cover?) and a pace (how long is it pertinent to negotiate?).

- Find the right framing. It is different to say, "You do not deserve to see the kids" than saying "You can see the kids, but you need to demonstrate that you have not been drunk in a while."

- Know and understand the legal terms that are important to you and your spouse.

- Have a good team. It is important that you have a preparation session, even if short, with your lawyer.

FORESIGHT

An ideal negotiation is not one where you and your spouse get what each wants today. It is a negotiation where all parties, including your kids, get the best long-term agreement. When negotiating, make sure that your side of the equation is calculated correctly. Always remember that the fact that something is less valuable to you today does not mean that it is less valuable to everybody now or in the future. Consider creative trade-offs and re-assess frequently what you should be fighting for.

APPENDIX 4: DOCUMENTS FOR INTERNATIONAL DIVORCE CASES

NOT FUN, BUT SOMETIMES NECESSARY.

STAY EXTENSION REQUEST TEMPLATE (FOREIGN FAMILY MEMBER)

MMM DD, YYYY
ADDRESS
CITY, STATE ZIP CODE
To: USCIS
Subject: Application to Extend Nonimmigrant Status (B-2)

Dear Officer,

I respectfully submit this extension request with the purpose to help my [RELATION TO PERSON] take care of her children [AGE 1 and AGE 2]. He/She is divorcing [filed on DATE]. I am the only person that can come help and he/she needs me for a few more months/days/weeks. My close and extended family lives in COUNTRY, all my assets and activity are in COUNTRY, this is a temporary visit to help. I am a [PROFESSION/RETIREE] and can sustain myself with my pension/assets until this temporary visit ends. My [RELATION TO PERSON] has income to cover my living as well, if needed. I will be staying at her/his house.

Thank you in advance for the attention provided to this letter.

Respectful regards,

_____

Mr. /Mr. First Name Last Name

P.S. Divorce petition is attached.

OPPOSITION TO CHILDREN'S PASSPORT ISSUANCE TEMPLATE

Mr. Ms. First Name Last Name

Your ADDRESS

CITY, STATE ZIP CODE

To

Honorable Consul of [COUNTRY] in [CITY]

[MMM DD, YYYY]

Subject : Disagreement to the Issuance of Passport or Travel Documents

Dear Consul,

I regret to share that on [MMM DD, YYYY] I filed a divorce petition from my spouse [First Name LAST NAME] in the [#] District court of [STATE] in [CITY].

Both, my spouse and I, currently reside in [CITY]. The standing order for the case orders us to refrain from removing the children from the state of [STATE].

We have two children :

[First Name LAST NAME]

[First Name LAST NAME]

[FIRST NAME] has an American and [NATIONALITY] birth certificate. [FIRST NAME] has an American and [NATIONALITY] birth certificate.

Through this letter I respectfully express my disagreement to the issuance or delivery of a [COUNTRY] Passport or any travel documentation to both of my children without my express authorization. This in pursuance to the procedure shared with me when I called the consulate on [MMM, DD, YYYY]. Additionally, I kindly request this disagreement to be registered by the concerned services and to be distributed to other Consulates or pertinent agencies, to the extent such distribution is offered by the Consulate.

If a passport has already been issued to either of my children, I kindly ask to be informed.

This action is not to represent a denial of the children's natural [COUNTRY] heritage, it is rather a precaution which hopefully will disappear once a final judgment is decreed and the parental authority is defined, by agreement or trial, and validated by the American and [COUNTRY] courts.

For reference please find enclosed the below documentation:

- Copy of the divorce petition

- Copy of my marriage certificate

- Copy of the STATE standing order

- Copy of [First Name LAST NAME FIRST CHILD] and [First Name LAST NAME SECOND CHILD] birth certificates

- Copy of my passport

I thank you in advance for your attention and remain at your disposition for any inquiries.

Kind Regards,

[First Name LAST NAME]

Notary Public [BEFORE SENDING, SIGN LETTER INFRONT OF NOTARY]

(STATE OF STATE   )

(COUNTY OF _____   )

Before me, the undersigned authority, came the principal who is of sound mind and eighteen (18) years of age, or older, and acknowledged that he voluntarily dated and signed this writing or directed to be dated and signed as above.

Done this_____day of _____, 20_____.

Signature of Notary Public : _____

Date commission expires :_____

Appendix 5 Visitation Record keeping Template

MANY REGRET KEEPING NO RECORDS WHEN PROBLEMS ARISE.

The goal is to have a document that can be easily summarized. Excel can be a great tool. However, if it is difficult to access a computer, you can also use a general-purpose agenda or notebook. Summarizing will be tough, but it is better than nothing.

A template created within Excel can have the below column titles. Keep the entries consistent so that you can use filters and PivotTables. The web has several videos showing how to easily use these Excel tools.

- Date

- Weekend? (Y/N)

- Extended Period? (Y/N)

- Parent came? (Y/N)

- Parent was on time? (Y/N)

- Parent brought back kids on time? (Y/N)

- Parent did pick up? (Y/N)

- Parent did drop off? (Y/N)

- Friendly interaction with spouse? (Y/N)

- Notes? (Y/N)

APPENDIX 6: RECOMMENDED BOOKS

ALSO GOOD FOR FALLING ASLEEP QUICKLY AFTER A LONG DAY.

Below I share the titles that I liked the most by category. They were all very helpful.

1. Empowering

   • "The Nice Girl Syndrome, 10 steps to empowering yourself and ending abuse" by Beverly Engel

   • "The Catholic's Divorce Survival Guide, Helping You Find Peace, Power, and Passion After Your Divorce." It was helpful for me; the principles and path given are quite universal.

2. About the impact of divorce on children

   • "The Unexpected Legacy of Divorce, the 25-year landmark study" by Judith S. Wallerstein, Julia M. Lewis, and Sandra Blakeslee

   • "Between Two Worlds, The Inner Lives of Children of Divorce" by Elizabeth Marquardt

3. Co-parenting

   • "Joint Custody with a Jerk, Raising A Child with an Uncooperative Ex" by Julie a. Ross., M.A. and Judy Corcoran

- "Putting Children First, Proven Parenting Strategies for Helping Children Thrive Through Divorce" by Joanne Pedro-Carroll, Ph.D.

Links to useful articles and websites, particularly about the legal process, jurisdiction, custody, division of property, international considerations and the like, can be found at:

www.mydivorcehandbook.com

Most of the content is focused on Texas.

GLOSSARY

THE EXCRUCIATING LEGALESE MADE SIMPLE...

Alimony. Husband's or wife's court-ordered provision for a spouse after separation or divorce. It is an amount of money that one spouse, who can pay, gives to the other on a regular basis, if he/she is unable to satisfy his/her financial needs.

Apostille. A seal, issued by a government in accordance with the Hague Convention, certifying a document as official and enforceable in its territory. The seal permits the presentation of such document in another country to seek the continuation of its legal effect there.

Appeal. When a party is unsatisfied with the outcome and asks the court to reconsider based on argumentations. A person can Appeal a divorce only if the terms of it were decided by the court (there was no Settlement Agreement or Mediated Agreement between the spouses). Additionally, such Appeal should argue that the court did not apply the law correctly (it is not that you have new evidence or the like). Appeals can be filed within certain timeframes and there are rules directing how and for what an Appeal can be done.

Bond. A Bond is an agreement by which a person guarantees that he or she will do certain act. Failure to perform the act obligates the person to pay a sum of money or forfeit money on deposit. Usually purchased from a third party (a "bondsman"). This third party will pay in full the bonded amount if the person fails to perform.

Child Support. Court-ordered payments, typically made by a non-Custodial Parent, to support one's minor child or children.

Community Property State. The assumption at marriage is that the community property (marriage property) belongs to both spouses, independently of who earned or bought the property. Community Property is to be distributed equally between the spouses (absent a Prenuptial or Postnuptial Agreement, Fault or other attenuating circumstances; your lawyer will know what is applicable to you). In general terms (with some exceptions) gifts from one spouse to the other, inheritances and property that was separate before marriage are not community property. The rest is, even if acquired under the name of a one spouse.

Conservator. A person or parent that has parenting and Possession (full or partial) rights over the children.

Conservatorship. A concept used to describe the rights and obligations Conservators have over the children.

Contested Divorce. A divorce where the spouses cannot agree, either on getting divorced or on the terms of the divorce.

Custodian or Custodial Parent. A person that has custody of a child.

Custody. The right to have Possession of a child. An individual can have full or partial Custody. However, outside of the legal world, it is said that the person that has more Possession of the children has Custody, even though such Custody is partial if the other parent has overnight Visitation rights.

Decree. An official order from a court. In a divorce case the order is expressed in a written document that contains all the terms of the divorce, along with the signatures of the spouses, lawyers and the Judge.

Deed of Trust to Secure Assumption. A document that, when used in conjunction with the Warranty Deed, has the effect of releasing the spouse that gave up ownership of a property of the mortgage payments of such property. This does not mean that the spouse is no longer in the loan, what it means is that, if the new owner does not pay, then the spouse that gave up the property can foreclose or take over payments (and consequently ownership of the portion he/she starts paying).

Divorce Decree or Decree. A decree is an official order issued by a family law judge where the judge says that the spouses are divorced. Within the document the judge also details what is the division of property, what is the Child Support and the child Custody terms.

Divorce Petition. Document filed in court where one of the spouses lets the court know that he/she wants to divorce the other spouse. It contains a lot of detail including, but not limited to: names and ages of the spouses and children, residency, petition for temporary visiting schedule, how health care will be managed, etc.

Equitable Distribution State. Equitable property means that each property is owned by the person that earned such property (it usually means that you can trace who purchased the asset or that the asset is property of only one of the spouses). Equitable distribution states are to distribute property in a "fair and equitable" way (commensurate with the circumstances of the divorce). You can go to court and try to prove that there was a verbal agreement that the property was of both, but it is difficult to do.

Exequatur. Legal document issued by a sovereign authority (usually a government's judicial branch) that permits the exercise or enforcement of a right within the Jurisdiction of the authority (country).

Fault. A spouse taking an action that goes against the agreements and legal promises made when getting married.

Fault Divorce. As the name indicates, it is a divorce where one spouse claims that the other did something wrong that should have legal consequences (sometimes economical). In a Fault Divorce, if the process happens quickly (which sometimes might not be the case), you can get a divorce without being subject to the Waiting Period. Fault Divorces are usually costlier, as one party is usually very defensive as the consequences can be big.

Hague Convention. An international treaty, signed by several countries, that creates international rules and processes to address a multitude of topics. Key amongst those topics is child abduction. The convention provides an expeditious method to return a child that has been abducted by a parent, if the child were to be taken away from his usual place of residence.

Hearing. The opportunity to present to the court an issue and ask for its help to resolve it (permanently or temporarily).

Jurisdiction. Even though the U.S. is a single country, states have different laws and procedures. With so many laws in the United States (and in the world!), the legal systems had to create rules to define which court has the right to hear and decide a case (which court has the "official power to make a legal decision or judgment"). When a court is entitled to decide a case, that court has "Jurisdiction". For example, a simple rule could be: If any of the two spouses lived in a state during the previous 6 months, without interruption, then such state's court can decide the case. So, what if you and your spouse, for some reason, lived for 6 months in different states? Well, in general terms, both states have Jurisdiction. In the U.S., the court that receives the case first usually becomes the court with exclusive Jurisdiction. When the courts of two countries could be involved, it is best to understand the potential Jurisdiction scenarios before filing for divorce.

Mediated Agreement. Agreement reached by the spouses with the help of a Mediator. It is an initial document, usually not yet fully drafted, wherein the parties express their agreements. Both spouses sign such document. The document is later "cleaned-up." Additional language that clarifies what was agreed is later added.

Mediation. A form of alternative dispute resolution in which the spouses meet with a neutral third-party in an effort to settle the case. The third-party is called a mediator.

Monitoring Fee. In Texas, Custodial Parents who receive full-service monitoring and enforcement services and have never received temporary assistance for needy families are charged a service fee (approximately $25 USD) for each year that they receive at least $500 in Child Support collections. The fee is deducted from the Child Support payment (thus why your Decree must ask that the parent giving support pays it).

Motion to Modify. This is when you ask the court to modify the terms of the divorce, usually because of a change of circumstances. For example: If the primary care giver is now on drugs, the other spouse can ask to become the primary care giver.

No Fault Divorce. Neither spouse blames the other. Equates to what is widely known as "irreconcilable differences." Filing a No-Fault Divorce does not mean that there will not be a negotiation or that you will agree to everything. Courts can still decide topics on a No Fault Divorce. A No Fault Divorce usually requires the spouses to live apart for a certain period of time before granting divorce.

Prenuptial Agreement. A contract that was signed to modify the way that the marriage will work. It usually has clauses that define how the spouses will manage the separation of assets if divorce occurs.

Possession. The fact of having an asset or a child physically. The term "use and possession" is usually utilized to describe assets and who has control over them. In the case of children, it refers to the periods of time when the children are with one of the parents or Conservators ("a child is in possession of the mother").

Postnuptial Agreement. A contract that was signed after marriage, while the spouses are still married. It usually has clauses that define how the spouses will manage the separation of assets if divorce occurs.

Power of Attorney. A legal document giving power of attorney to someone. Power of attorney is the authority to act for another person.

Process Server. A person, especially a sheriff or deputy, who serves (gives, delivers) writs, warrants, subpoenas, copies of the divorce petition, etc.

Protective Order. It is a court order that protects you from someone who has been abusive, violent or threatened to be violent. Violence can include sexual assault. It usually requires a person to remain away or not contact another person.

Residency Requirements. The spouses have to live for a defined period of time within the boundaries of a court, in order to file there. The same applies for the children. The children have to live for a defined period of time within the boundaries of a given court, in order for that court to decide the case.

Service. The formal delivery of a document, usually by a Process Server.

Settlement Agreement. A written document that records or memorializes agreements reached by the spouses with the help of their lawyers.

Settlement Offer. As in a business transaction, it is an offer where each spouse indicates the terms that he is willing to agree in order to close the divorce, without going to trial.

Standard Possession Order. It varies state by state. This order details a Visitation schedule that the court deems to work, generally, in the best interest of the children.

Standing Order. Some counties have orders that automatically kick in when a Divorce Petition is filed. These orders automatically prohibit both spouses from taking certain actions upon filing of the divorce case. Unless one of the spouses requests a modification of it, those orders are in place while the divorce is happening. Violating such orders has legal consequences.

Substantial Connections. The law sees this item differently by court and country. What makes a connection "substantial?" Is it that the person lived in a place for a long time? Maybe the origins of the family have always been elsewhere and the person considers that place home, even though most of the time he/she lived abroad? The determination of what is a substantial connection can be subjective. Especially if the person has meaningful connections to more than one place.

Temporary Orders. A decision from the court that has temporary effect. For example, one of the counsels can request the court to issue a temporary order to solve an urgent matter before the first divorce Hearing takes place.

Trust Fund. Lawyers usually ask you to pre-pay a certain number of hours. All pre-payments you do go to a "Trust Fund," which can be seen as a sort of checking account from which your lawyer can withdraw money. The particularity of this "checking account" is that it contains your money. As a result, if the lawyer does not work in your case, he cannot withdraw any money. In fact, at the end of your case, if there is leftover money, he has to give the money back to you.

Uncontested Divorce. There are always disagreements, but usually it is best when the spouses are able to agree without going to the Judge. An Uncontested Divorce is a divorce where all items are agreed without the help of the Judge. The court and the legal steps just make the divorce official.

Visitation. The time a divorced person, who is not the primary Custodian, spends with his/her children.

Waiting Period. Once divorce is filed, the courts stipulate that the spouses shall wait a set amount of time before going to court. This does not mean that nothing happens. The courts hope that such time is used to advance negotiations or resolve issues outside of court.

Waiver of Service. A document that a spouse signs where he acknowledges being notified about and receiving the divorce filing documents, without being formally served by a Process Server.

Warranty Deed. A document with which a person transfers ownership of a property guaranteeing that such property has a clear owner.

About The Author

Camille Cardelus is the pen name of the author. She is working mom currently holding a senior management position within a major U.S. corporation. She wrote the No-nonsense Divorce Handbook to help other busy parents throughout their journey.

Made in the USA
Columbia, SC
10 February 2025

53627962R00062